DISCOV
HAWAII
The Aloha State

Text by
STU DAWRS

Photography by
ANN CECIL
·
RON DAHLQUIST
·
PHILIP ROSENBERG

Page 1: *Snorkeling at Hanauma Bay, O'ahu. This page, clockwise from top left: Hā'ena Beach, Kaua'i. Best friends. Radio telescope, Mauna Kea, the Big Island. Fisherman gathers his net, Kaua'i. Molten lava, the Big Island. Palms silhouetted against the West Maui Mountains, seen from Lahaina. Hula dancer at sunset, Waikīkī. Green and white anthurium. Opposite, clockwise from top left: King Kamehameha statue with leis, O'ahu. The Nā Pali Coast, Kaua'i. The ancient Hawaiian art of chanting. Pink plumeria. Ni'ihau shell leis. Wailua Falls, Kaua'i. Jacob and Angel Mau share a special moment, Maui. Moon setting over Maui. Lava flow to the Pacific, Volcanoes park.*

CONTENTS

E KOMO MAI

WELCOME!

"HAWAI'I IS THE 50TH STATE." There is probably no statement of fact that is simultaneously more obvious and more misleading. True, Hawai'i became a state in 1959, a mere 66 years after the island chain's ruling monarch, Queen Lili'uokalani, was forcibly overthrown. But, aside from the outward trappings of statehood, there is little to identify The Aloha State with the rest of the union.

The only state to be surrounded by water; the state that boasts the world's most continuously active volcano; one of the remotest populated spots on earth . . . Hawai'i is set apart in the simplest of geographic terms.

The differences also run on a deeper level. Hawai'i is the only state to once have had a ruling monarch. The first inhabitants of these islands crossed thousands of miles of uncharted ocean to reach a land they had no way of knowing even existed. Many of Hawai'i's more recent settlers arrived knowing little more about their destination than did the earliest islanders. Laborers brought in from China, Japan, the Philippines, Portugal and throughout Europe to work the sugar cane fields in the late 19th century would forever alter the social framework of the islands.

Eastbound on Honolulu's H-1 freeway during rush hour, it seems that all of Hawai'i is changing in a rush. Though these islands are millions of years old, the first Polynesian seafarers set foot here a relatively scant 1,500 years ago. The islands were "discovered" again by Captain James Cook in 1778. Since then, it seems that everything has changed—and rapidly. A little more than a century after Cook first made sight of O'ahu and Kaua'i, the islands had been united for the first time under King Kamehameha I; the traditional Hawaiian pantheon of gods had been all but abandoned by Kamehameha II; private land ownership had been instigated; Hawai'i's queen had been dethroned and native Hawaiians were on their way to becoming a minority in their own land—the native population having declined by nearly 85 percent, due mainly to introduced diseases. Today, some estimate that the population of urban Honolulu alone is greater than that of the entire island chain at the time of Cook's arrival.

Things change quickly and they don't. Driving another route, Maui's Hāna Highway, one is reminded of other, slower days. Carved out of the island's northeastern coastline in 1927 using only picks and shovels,

Preceding pages: Ulua Beach, Maui, the island with the most swimmable beaches in Hawai'i.
Above: Hikers on the Kalalau Trail admiring the view of the Nā Pali Coast, Kaua'i.
Background: Looking out to Chinaman's Hat over
the Kahalu'u fishpond, windward O'ahu.

the road traverses 52 miles between Pā'ia and Hāna, snaking its way through some 600 turns and across more than 50 one-lane bridges. Rounding any given hairpin corner, motorists are alternately greeted by sheer drops to the ocean, sometimes hundreds of feet below, and cascading waterfalls dropping through the backs of steep valleys.

Throughout Hawai'i there are reminders of a past that is not so far removed. On every island one can find sacred heiau (temples) and pu'uhonua—places of refuge. The most famous of these, Pu'uhonua o Hōnaunau, still stands 22 miles south of modern-day Kailua-Kona, on the island of Hawai'i. Built sometime around the year 1550, Pu'uhonua o Hōnaunau is a wonder. Like all rock constructions of ancient Hawai'i, the wall that surrounds this place of refuge is made of stones that are held together solely by friction—no

mortar was used. Phenomenal when one considers the dimensions of the great wall: 10 feet high, 17 feet wide and 1,000 feet long.

And change occurs even more slowly. Kīlauea volcano, also on the island of Hawai'i, has been erupting almost continuously since 1983. In its long march to the sea, the volcano goddess Pele's lava has been both a builder and a destroyer—creating miles of new coastline even as it has forced residents to abandon the town of Kalapana and watch helplessly as more than 150 homes were inundated and burnt to the ground.

In recent years, change has taken other forms. Since the mid-1970s, Hawaiian culture has been going through what many refer to as a renaissance. While Hawaiian students were once beaten for speaking their native language in public, today Hawaiian immersion schools are helping young islanders to preserve their

language. Likewise, traditional arts like hula, weaving and carving, and sports like outrigger canoe paddling have all experienced a resurgence.

Things change and things remain the same. Through all of the transformations that Hawai'i has seen, one thing has remained constant—the nearly undefinable quality known simply as the aloha spirit. It is an essence that takes many forms, and seems to quite literally spring from the land and sea. Simply put, it is everywhere, but perhaps most of all it is in the people who live here. Surrounded on all sides by water, in one of the remotest spots on earth, the people who inhabit these islands share a common bond—a love and respect for the land and each other. This more than anything else makes Hawai'i what it is—the 50th state, the Aloha state . . . and a land like no other on earth.

E komo mai. Welcome to Hawai'i.

Opposite: Ālau Island as seen from Koki Beach, Hāna, Maui. Above: Canoe club paddlers practice for long distance races off Hōnaunau on the Kona Coast of the Big Island. Right: Ki'i— wooden images of gods—at the Place of Refuge, Hōnaunau.

HĀNAU

BIRTH

THE VOLCANIC CONES that form the Hawaiian islands are among the most massive natural structures on earth—and the most prodigious. Although the area which most people refer to as Hawai'i covers a mere 400 miles and is comprised of eight islands, this area is only the southeastern end of a very long lei. The Hawaiian archipelago is in truth a volcanic necklace of some 130 islands, islets and shoals that stretch 1,600 miles across the North Pacific.

Every island in the Hawaiian chain was created by a single "hot spot" in the earth's mantle. It is estimated that, for as long as 100 million years, the plate of the earth's crust that lies beneath the Pacific Ocean has been migrating northwest over this superheated vent, traveling at approximately four inches per year. Meanwhile, the hot spot has remained stationary, thereby creating a string of islands that stretches from the oldest formations (the submerged Emperor Seamounts at the northwest end of the Hawaiian chain) to the site of the hot spot's current activity—the island of Hawai'i, at the southeastern end of the chain.

Because of the vast variance in age among the islands, each has a slightly different look and feel. At one time or another, however, all had the same basic shape—that of a warrior's shield. This is because each was originally formed by one or more "shield" volcanoes. Haleakalā on Maui, rising 10,023 feet above sea-level and nearly 30,000 feet from the ocean floor, is still a nearly intact shield volcano, as are Mauna Kea and Mauna Loa on the island of Hawai'i. Olokele, the volcano that formed Kaua'i, has long since been weathered down to what is now known as Mount Wai'ale'ale —at 5,148 feet, the peak has been so heavily eroded that it is hard to imagine it was once nearly twice its current height.

Because of the varying effects of erosion, each of the major Hawaiian islands is a geologist's dream; each is in a different phase of geologic growth or decay. Kaua'i, the eldest of the major islands, has a face that has been immensely weathered—the Waimea Canyon and Nā Pali coastline at times plunge thousands of vertical feet. The island of Hawai'i, the youngest, is literally still growing, with Kīlauea volcano adding hundreds of acres of new land in recent decades.

Erosion isn't the only force that has shaped these islands. While Maui today covers roughly 728 square miles, the island was once, during the glacial period, roughly four times its present size. Maui-nui, as this ancient island is sometimes referred to, was estimated to be 3,230 square miles. As the polar caps melted and sea levels rose, the low-points on this large island were submerged, forming the separate islands of Maui, Lāna'i, Moloka'i, Kaho'olawe and Molokini.

And while erosion has long been credited for most

Above: *Molten lava covers Kamoamoa black sand beach in Hawai'i Volcanoes National Park.*
Background: *Visitors are amazed when lava pours into the Pacific and creates powerful explosions of light and sound.*

Opposite: *The view from the Nuʻuanu Pali Lookout, Oʻahu.*

Above: *The Koʻolau Mountains from the windward side of Oʻahu.*

of the major land features in the Islands, a more recent theory has been posited to explain the soaring cliffs known as "pali" which are found on nearly every island. It is now believed by some that massive landslides played a major role in shaping the islands.

Among the most dramatic of these cliffs is Oʻahu's Nuʻuanu Pali. Stretching for miles and soaring thousands of feet, there are actually two competing theories to explain the dramatic vertical walls on the windward side of the pali. Until fairly recently, it was believed that the cliffs were simply the result of headward erosion— that, over time, a series of valleys eroded westward until each valley head met to form one continuous cliff face.

However, in the mid-1960s, a geologist named James G. Moore put forth a more radical theory. It was Moore's belief that huge landslides (similar to the one that occurred at Washington State's Mount St. Helens in 1980, though on a much larger scale) played as

important a part as erosion in the shaping of at least some of the major land forms in the Hawaiian Islands, including the Nuʻuanu Pali.

It wasn't until nearly 20 years later, in 1983, that Moore would get a chance to prove his theory. It was in that year that U.S. president Ronald Reagan claimed sovereignty for the United States over all seabed resources within a 230-mile zone surrounding the United States—including, naturally, the 50th state. Having no idea what these resources were actually comprised of, the U.S. Geological Survey began an extensive mapping of the Hawaiian ridge—the 1,364 mile long, 372 mile wide, 507,000 square mile perch upon which the entire Hawaiian chain sits. What the surveyors came across was extraordinary: Debris on the sea floor indicated more than 68 major landslides measuring 12 miles or more in length between Midway Island to the northwest and the island of Hawaiʻi.

Eighty-seven miles offshore of Kaua'i's Nā Pali coast, scientists found debris that suggested a 62 mile wide, five million year old avalanche was responsible for carving out much of that jagged coastline.

If Moore's theory is correct, this type of avalanche took place on an even grander scale on O'ahu. The cliffs rising up behind the windward towns of Kāne'ohe and Kailua are believed to be the eroded back wall of an ancient volcanic crater, the other half of which literally broke off and tumbled into the sea. Proponents of the "Nu'uanu Slide" say there could be no other explanation for stone blocks up to 19 miles across and 11 miles wide that have been found as far as 30 miles offshore—an explanation that means the slide would have been more than 1,000 times larger than that at Mount St. Helens.

If this theory is true, scientists say, it could also account for such anomalies as coral deposits which have been found at elevations of more than 1,000 feet on the Island of Moloka'i. A major slide on the Kona coast of the island of Hawai'i about 100,000 years ago is thought to have created a tidal wave so large that it is barely imaginable—a wall of water over 1,000 feet tall.

Eruption, erosion, avalanche, evolution—every island in Hawai'i is in a state of constant flux. Though the eldest, Kaua'i, no longer features active volcanoes, it is constantly being carved away by waters flowing down from the summit of Mount Wai'ale'ale—the wettest spot on earth. Fifteen miles off the southeast coast of the Big Island, the youngest of the islands has yet to make an appearance. Still 3,000 feet below the surface, Lō'ihi volcano has risen more than 10,000 feet above the ocean floor, creating a caldera that measures close to three miles across. While it will be many thousand more years before Lō'ihi sees the light of day, the volcano continues to bubble in the black depths, reenacting a process that is millions of years old—*the birth of an island.*

Honopū Beach on the Nā Pali Coast of Kaua'i.

THE SEPARATE KINGDOM

THE ISLAND OF KAUA'I

THE SEPARATE KINGDOM. The Unconquerable Island. Kaua'i took these names after Kamehameha I twice failed to subjugate the island by force in the late 1700s. However, the island has always been a place apart. According to ancient lore, Pele the fire goddess was among the first to set foot on Kaua'i. When she left Kawiki Nui (that is, Tahiti) in search of a new home, the first large island she set foot on was Kaua'i. Unfortunately for her, there was no spot on the island deep enough to protect her fires from the sea goddess Namakao-kaha'i (Pele's sister), who was angry with Pele for seducing her lover and so pursued the volcano goddess across the Pacific, filling her craters with sea water and washing out Pele's fires. And so she moved on, eventually making her way to her present, spacious living quarters in Halema'uma'u Crater on the island of Hawai'i. This tale is still told throughout the Pacific to explain why craters like Olokele, the volcano that formed Kaua'i, have long been extinct while vents on the Big Island continue to spew lava to this day.

It is believed that Marquesans crossed some 2,000 miles of the Pacific Ocean to be the first humans to discover the Hawaiian Islands, somewhere near 500 A.D. Their first settlements were established near 750 A.D., quite possibly on Kaua'i. Because the island was settled so early in Hawai'i's history, and also perhaps because of its remoteness from the other islands in the chain, the royal bloodline of Kaua'i was thought by many to be among the purest, and its chieftains were considered some of the most sacred. Indeed, the story goes that Pele herself once fell in love with Lohiau, a handsome and powerful Kaua'i chief. But Pele did not create this island, and long before she made her fabled journey, Kaua'i would have broken the surface of the Pacific Ocean.

Whether one chooses to believe the mythic or scientific accounts, every island in the Hawaiian chain has a common origin. According to the *Kumulipo*, a 2,077-line genealogical chant that recounts the creation of the world, the islands were created by the union of Wākea the Sky-Father and Papa the Earth-Mother. The islands are literally children of the gods. The more pragmatic explanation has it that Kaua'i, like the rest of the islands in the chain, was formed by volcanic activity—in this case by the long-extinct Olokele. According to most estimates, Olokele first began erupting at least 10 million years ago; after rising nearly three miles, the lava broke the surface of the ocean several million years ago.

Today, remnants of Olokele make up the island's most impressive single feature—5,148 foot tall Mount

Above: *Heiau in Lydgate Park, Wailua River area, Kaua'i.*
Background: *Lush greenery surrounding a tour boat on the Wailua River.*

Wai'ale'ale (which literally translates as "rippling waters"). For most of the year, Wai'ale'ale's summit is shrouded in clouds, which led the island's earliest inhabitants to believe that the gods met beneath this misty cloak to determine the fate of the islands. In a very real sense, Wai'ale'ale's hidden peaks *do* determine much of what happens on Kaua'i. This area receives an average of 460 inches of rainfall per year, making it the wettest spot on earth and feeding the rivers, waterfalls and lush vegetation of the island's lower reaches. (Like all islands though, the rain can be localized. Some areas a mere 20 miles away receive less than 20 inches of rain per year.)

The once-fiery crater at the top of Wai'ale'ale is now the Alaka'i Swamp. Thirteen miles across and 30 square miles in total, Alaka'i is the largest high-elevation swamp in the world; its seven rivers trail out and down in all directions to the sea. One of these rivers, Waimea ("reddish water"), is the longest river in Hawai'i. This maze of rivers, streams and waterfalls has led in part to Kaua'i's more popular nickname—The Garden Isle.

As the eldest of the major Hawaiian islands, Kaua'i is the island that most shows its age. On every side, one sees the effects of erosion at work. Olokele volcano once pushed more than 10,000 feet into the heavens. Today the mountain has been eroded down to two main peaks that were once a part of its eastern flank—

Wai'ale'ale and Kawaikini (the island's highest point, at 5,243 feet). The rest of the mountain sank and formed the crater which houses Alaka'i Swamp.

Waimea Canyon, often referred to as the Grand Canyon of the Pacific, occupies 14 miles on the island's west end. Its deep, rain-carved valleys and craggy spires give ample credence to the nickname. To the north, the Nā Pali coast encompasses some 15 miles of nearly impassable terrain. Nā Pali rise thousands of feet out of the sea, in many places making a sheer vertical drop to the water below.

At approximately the same time that Kaua'i broke the surface, the island of Ni'ihau rose up 17.2 miles away across a shallow ocean channel. (Some speculate that the island may have been a part of Kaua'i at one time.) After millennia of erosion, Kaua'i has reached its present state—33 miles long and 25 miles wide at its widest points, with an area of 627 miles (and 90 miles of coastline).

Kaua'i did not come by its Separate Kingdom moniker easily. It was the only island able to withstand the forces of Kamehameha I as he swept through the rest of the chain, conquering six of the other seven inhabited islands and uniting them under one monarch for the first time in Hawai'i's history. In part, the island was saved by its remoteness from the others—Kamehameha's first attempt at conquest, in 1796, was thwarted by a storm in the channel between O'ahu

Opposite: *Waterfall tumbling down from Mt. Wai'ale'ale.*
Right: *The jagged cliffs and Mt. Wai'ale'ale on a rare cloudless day for the mountain.*

Above: *Along the road to Kōkeʻe and Waimea Canyon.* Below: *Contours of Waimea Canyon.*

Right: *The Iliau plant along the rim of Waimea Canyon, "the Grand Canyon of the Pacific."*

Scenes from Kaua'i's north shore.
Opposite, top to bottom and
left to right: People relaxing
in the central area of Hanalei.
Road into Hanalei. Looking
toward the center of Hanalei.
Pu'u Pōā Beach at Princeville.
Quiet moments in Hanalei.
Above: A summer afternoon
at the beach, Hanalei Bay.
Rainbows over Hanalei
Valley. Left: Windsurfing near
Hā'ena Beach. Right: The
Ching Young Store, Hanalei.
Pages 24–25: Spouting Horn
in the Po'ipū Beach region.

and Kaua'i. Eight years later, Kamehameha would try again, but this time the adverse effects of Western contact would backhandedly benefit the island, when an illness (most likely cholera) decimated the attackers.

For all its remoteness, Kaua'i, over the centuries, has been an island of firsts. Nearly 20 years before Kamehameha would attempt his Kaua'i attacks, Captain James Cook would make the first known landfall by a westerner in Hawai'i, anchoring his *Resolution* and *Discovery* at Waimea, on Kaua'i's southwest coast, on January 20, 1778.

In 1835, Ladd and Company leased a tract of land in the island's southeastern Kōloa area from Kamehameha III to grow cane—a crop that had been brought by Hawai'i's earliest groups of Polynesians settlers. The first sugar in Hawai'i was produced in 1802 by Chinese immigrants on the island of Lāna'i, but the sugar that would be produced at Kōloa was the first to be commercially exported from Hawai'i.

Later, the effects of this first export would be seen

throughout the islands, as foreign (that is, American) sugar growers became increasingly influential in Hawaiian government—eventually becoming one of the driving forces behind the unlawful overthrow of Queen Lili'uokalani on O'ahu in 1893 and Hawai'i's subsequent annexation by the United States . . . and even, to a lesser extent, the push toward Statehood in 1959.

These were the long-term effects of sugar. In the short term, the Kōloa plantation brought about other changes. In ancient times Wailua, on the island's east coast, was the religious capital of Kaua'i, while Waimea was the more secular capital. Once Kōloa started importing equipment for its mill and later exporting sugar, the tiny Kōloa Landing became the major port on the island—and would remain so for nearly a century. The town that sprung up around the mill became a major population center.

Like Lahaina on Maui and Honolulu on O'ahu, Kōloa was also affected (albeit briefly) by the whaling industry. Beginning circa 1830, peaking in the early

1840s and declining by 1860, the whaling industry further transported Kōloa Landing—to this day, some still refer to the area as "Whaler's Cove."

And of course, Kōloa's sugar plantations would have another effect still visible today. Like the rest of Hawai'i, the lack of labor necessary to grow and harvest cane meant that laborers and field managers were imported from across the globe. Today, one of the remotest spots in the Pacific Ocean is inhabited not only by Hawaiians but by second and third generation families from China, Japan, the Philippines, Portugal, Puerto Rico and throughout Europe.

Though spots like Wailua and Waimea had been inhabited for centuries, other towns on Kaua'i didn't even emerge until the early decades of the 19th century. Līhu'e, for example, is not referred to in any historical texts until 1837. Prior to that, the main trail from Waimea to Wailua bypassed the area completely, traveling inland instead. Sugar, however, would transform the area. Today, Līhu'e is located just outside the island's main airport and is the island's county seat.

Like all of Hawai'i, Kaua'i is a mix of the modern and the timeless. Princeville's planned resort area on the island's north coast features its own airport; and yet, near Nāwiliwili Harbor on the island's southeast shore, one can still view the Alekoko Fishpond, said to

Opposite: *The old plantation town of Kōloa near Po'ipū Beach.*

Below: *Alakoko Menehune Fish Pond near Nāwiliwili Harbor.*

Pages 30–31: *Twin beaches of Honopū, Nā Pali Coast, Kaua'i.*

be built in times long forgotten by the legendary Menehune—a mysterious race of people who, according to popular legend, came out only at night, had prodigious strength and minimal height (supposedly standing in the two- to three-foot range).

In a way, this peculiar mix is the simplest way to give a sense of Kaua'i's magic. It lingers everywhere.

Today, the island can essentially be divided into four geographic areas: the north coast, running roughly from Hā'ena through Hanalei and Princeville to

Left: *Sunday services at the Anahola Baptist Church.* Below: *Anahola Beach on the northeastern shore of Kaua'i.*

Opposite: *Taro or "kalo" terraces at Limahuli Gardens, one of the National Tropical Botanical Gardens.*

Pages 32–33: *Kalalau Valley.*
This page, left, top to bottom:
Kalalau Beach, on the Nā
Pali Coast. One of the twin
beaches at Honopū. Waterfall
flowing into the Waimea River.
Above: *Golden afternoon*
light shines over the spectacular
cliffs along the Nā Pali Coast.

Kīlauea; the east coast, which encompasses the areas of Anahola, Kapaʻa and Wailua; the south coast, from Līhuʻe through Kōloa, Hanapēpē, Waimea town and out to the end of Highway 50 at Mānā; and the west and northwest coasts, dominated by the dual wonders of Waimea Canyon and the Nā Pali Coast. (Kauaʻi's "Belt Highway" is actually a broken chain—no road has been built to span the undulating grandeur of the Nā Pali coastline.)

The Separate Kingdom. To this day, Kauaʻi retains a feeling of separateness. Of the four main islands (the others being Oʻahu, Maui and Hawaiʻi), Kauaʻi—the eldest—has the smallest population. Born 10 million years ago, the product of the union of a god and a goddess, Kauaʻi to this day shows its divine lineage. It's a magic that is visible not only in the grandeur of Waimea Valley and the Nā Pali Coast, but in the faces of its inhabitants. It's a magic that isn't easily forgotten.

NĀ HOʻOKELE
THE NAVIGATORS

ALTHOUGH NO ONE knows exactly when the first Polynesian navigators landed on Hawaiʻi's shores, most date the intentional settlement by islanders from the south as taking place between 500 and 800 A.D. The islands were no doubt originally stumbled upon, but the incredible fact remains that the earliest navigators were able to find their way back and forth without instruments, using only the position of sun, moon and stars, cloud formations, the movements of fish, ocean currents and swell directions as guides to their destination. Having found these islands but no doubt ill-provisioned to settle them, the first of these navigators eventually returned home with tales of an uninhabited land of plenty to the north—tales that were preserved through ancient navigational chants in islands as far flung as Bora Bora, Moorea and Tahiti.

Numerous chants, stories and legends tell of repeated voyages between Hawaiʻi and Tahiti. Indeed, the name of the ocean channel that separates Maui, Kahoʻolawe and Lānaʻi suggests a strong link between the two island nations—Kealaikahiki translates literally as "the path to Tahiti." It is not hard to imagine Kealaikahiki pointing the way south to Tahiti for ancient mariners, just as it is reasonable to believe that massive Haleakalā would serve as a navigational point for north-bound sailors.

To understand the navigational prowess of Polynesia's ancient mariners, one needs to understand the sheer distances they were covering. The Hawaiian island chain is located at the extreme northern point of the Polynesian triangle, an area that is bounded on each side by legs extending more than 5,000 miles —southwest to New Zealand and southeast to Easter Island. (As further proof of the common roots of islanders throughout Polynesia, the language spoken on islands flung across the triangle is remarkably similar. For example, the word for an indigenous islander is "maori" in New Zealand, "maohi" in Tahiti and "maoli" in Hawaiʻi.)

It is generally agreed that Hawaiʻi was settled in two waves. The first planned migrations were from the islands that Spanish explorers called the Marquesas— 11 southern hemisphere islands on the extreme eastern edge of Polynesia, roughly midway between Hawaiʻi and Easter Island. Traveling in double-hulled canoes that ranged in length from 60 to 80 feet and that could comfortably carry up to 30 family members, these once fierce warriors continued to arrive for some 500 years, settling peacefully (there was no longer competition

Above: A weathered outrigger canoe, Moʻorea, French Polynesia. Background: An aerial view of the beautiful lagoon at Bora Bora. Opposite top: Big Beach, Mākena, East Maui. Opposite bottom: Paddlers off Sugar Beach, Kīhei, Maui.

for land) and abandoning such habits as eating the bodies of their defeated foes.

The second wave of settlers came from the center of the Polynesian triangle—from Tahiti—during the 12th century. The dominant Tahitians quickly subjugated the original settlers, introducing new gods and a rigid set of laws known as the *kapu* system. Travel between Tahiti and Hawai'i is believed to have continued for an estimated 100 years, before abruptly—and without explanation—ceasing.

At this point, Hawai'i for the most part disappeared from Polynesian consciousness, remaining isolated for nearly 500 years until Captain James Cook set foot on the island of Kaua'i in 1778—assuring that Hawai'i would never again be truly secluded, and opening the door for an ongoing wave of white settlers that would change the island nation forever.

Opposite: *Paddlers at sunset.*
Above: *Mt. Otemanu rises from the sea on the island of Bora Bora.*
Below: *An aerial view of southwest Maui's La Pérouse Bay and Āhihi-Kinau Natural Reserve.*

THE GATHERING PLACE
THE ISLAND OF O'AHU

THE GATHERING PLACE. One glance at downtown Honolulu's skyline and it's easy to see the relevance of O'ahu's nickname. Only the third largest of the Hawaiian Islands at 607 square miles, O'ahu's population of 870,000 comprises almost 80 percent of the entire island chain—with nearly 380,000 concentrated in the urban Honolulu area. The main campus of the University of Hawai'i, with its 18,000 full-time students, is located in Mānoa Valley, on the slopes above Waikīkī. The per capita population density of Makiki, an area just east of downtown, is comparable to that of Manhattan.

If one takes the narrowest interpretation, O'ahu proper technically no longer exists. This is because the entire island falls under the jurisdiction of the City and County of Honolulu—as do the more than 100 uninhabited islands and atolls that stretch across 1,600 miles to the northeast of Kaua'i, making Honolulu, in name at least, the largest "city" in the world.

While an O'ahu resident referring to "Honolulu" more often than not is talking about a narrowly defined area of southern O'ahu, Honolulu remains anchored in Hawai'i's collective psyche as a center. As example, it has only been in recent years that the other inhabited islands in the chain have managed to shake their common reference as the "outer islands" for the slightly more inclusive term "neighbor islands."

This was not always the case. As late as the turn of the 19th century, Honolulu was a dusty village with fewer than 300 grass huts to its name and a population that varied depending on how many foreign ships were anchored in its harbor. Through the late 1700s, O'ahu was an "outer island." Indeed, some say that the island's Gathering Place moniker stems less from its current population density than the fact that, in other times, it was far enough removed from the center of things to make it a neutral spot ideal for negotiations between opposing chiefs.

However, O'ahu possessed something that no other Hawaiian island did. Honolulu harbor was literally the only protected, deep-water harbor for thousands of miles. Not long after Captain James Cook had stumbled upon these islands on January 18, 1778 (when he first landed at Waimea on the island of Kaua'i), the face of O'ahu in particular and Hawai'i in general would change radically. After Cook's death on the Kona Coast of the island of Hawai'i in 1779, no other Western ship arrived until 1785. It is believed that Westerners didn't learn of Honolulu harbor until sometime in the early 1790s . . . but once they did find it, change was inevitable. Less than a decade later, Kamehameha I recognized that trade with Westerners was bringing about an alteration in the population patterns of the islands. In 1804, he moved his court to Honolulu;

Above and background: *The Aloha Tower, Honolulu.*
Opposite: *Above the Aloha Tower Marketplace,*
downtown Honolulu.

one of his heirs, Kamehameha III, would permanently establish the royal court there in the 1840s.

In the ensuing years, Honolulu would be witness to changes that would forever alter the course of Hawaiian history. One need only walk through a two-block area in downtown to guess at what these changes entailed. Within little more than a stone's throw of each other stand 'Iolani Palace (built in 1873–74), the Mission House Museum (1819–1821), the Kawaiaha'o Church (1836–1842) and the Hawaii State Capitol (1969). Though this same area is filled with numerous other historic buildings and sites, these four structures serve as a timeline and a metaphor for the major transformations that took place in the relatively brief period of Hawaiian history following Captain Cook's 1778 landfall—the unification of the islands under Kamehameha in the 1790s; the arrival of the first missionaries

Opposite: *The heart of down-town Honolulu, 'Iolani Palace and the open air State Capitol. Above: Aloha Tower. Right, top to bottom: Tamarind* *Square, downtown Honolulu. Tasting spicy soup in Chinatown. "Catch of the Day." Chinatown scene. Chinese New Year goodies for sale. Kawaiaha'o Church.*

in 1820; the overthrow of Queen Lili'uokalani in 1893 and the 1959 vote that led to Hawai'i's statehood.

Today, the effects of these events are readily appar-ent in all aspects of Honolulu life. One need only walk three blocks west of 'Iolani Palace to see how this has played out. From the palace grounds (now somewhat ironically dwarfed by the neighboring State Capitol building), one passes directly into the heart of Honolulu's banking district; from there, directly into the historic Chinatown area. . . .

The Gathering Place is now truly that—gathered in this three block area, one finds faces from every part of the globe and every social strata. It is a multi-ethnic, multi-cultural society afloat in the middle of the Pacific Ocean.

Left: *Aerial view—Waikīkī, the Ala Wai Canal, Diamond Head.* Below: *Royal Hawaiian Hotel.* Opposite top: *Afternoon around* the *Moana Hotel's Banyan Court and Beach Bar, Waikīkī.* Bottom: *Visitors, palms, Waikīkī Beach and Diamond Head.*

Just east of downtown is the famed (some would say infamous) Waikīkī. Few areas in Hawai'i have seen as many changes-of-face and outright reincarnations as has Waikīkī (which translates as "spouting water"). While as many as 80 percent of the people who visit the islands eventually end up spending at least one night here, the area's life as a tourist destination is a relatively new one. Prior to the construction of the Moana Hotel in 1901 (the completion of which raised a minor uproar because it interfered with the previously unobstructed view of Diamond Head), there were only a few small, beachfront hotels. At the time, the inshore areas of Waikīkī were comprised primarily of low-lying swampland fed by streams running off the

Ko'olau mountains. With the exception of a few highly exclusive vacation homes and the beach houses kept by Hawaiian royalty (the area was long one of the prime surfing spots for kings), Waikīkī was for the most part dedicated to aqua- and agriculture. There were fishponds here, as well as fields for taro, rice and bananas.

Barely five years after the Moana was completed, it was decided by Lucius Pinkham, the director of Hawai'i's Board of Health, that Waikīkī's swampy marshlands were "dangerous and unsanitary." Construction was thus commenced on the Ala Wai Canal, which, when completed in the early 1920s, was used to drain the area. Soil dredged up during the construction of the canal was used as landfill, and greater Waikīkī was born. Today, area residents, workers in the visitor industry and tourists themselves combine to give Waikīkī an average daily population of over 100,000 people, making it one of the most densely populated spots on earth.

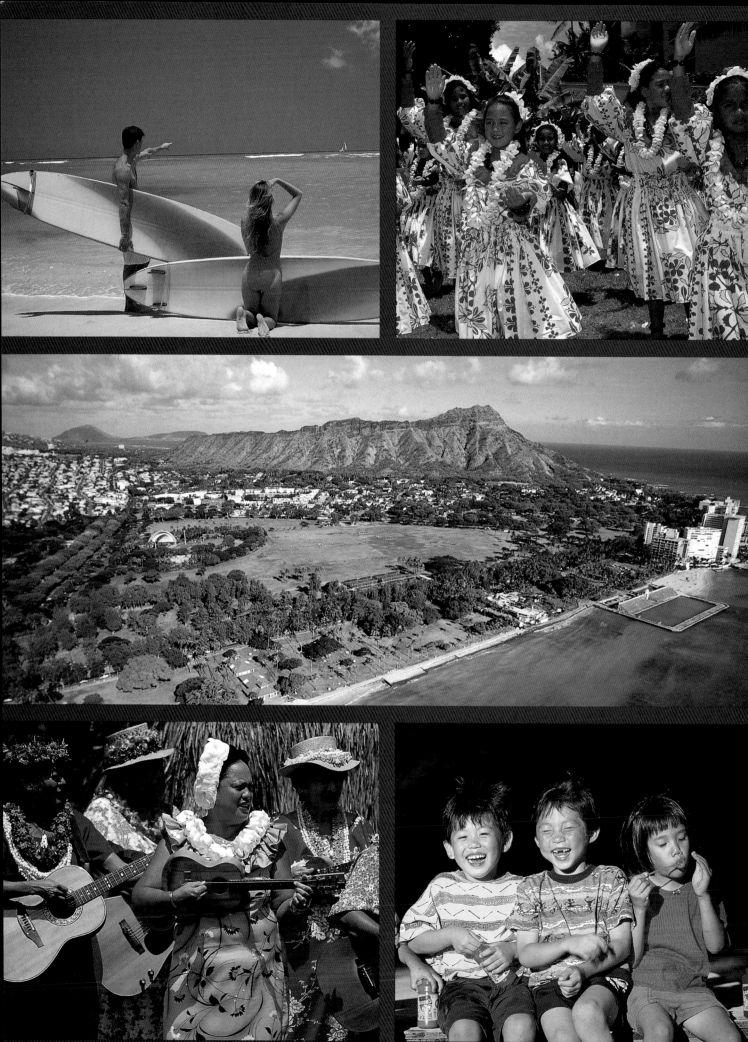

Kapi'olani Park and Waikīkī.
Opposite, top: Couple with
surfboards on beach near
Diamond Head. Keiki hula
dancers. Center: Aerial view
of Kapi'olani Park, Diamond
Head. Bottom: Dancers from
the Kodak Hula Show. Island
keiki (children) at play.
This page, clockwise from
top: Kite festival, Kapi'olani
Park. Mahimahi exhibit at
Waikīkī Aquarium. Kodak
Hula Show. 'Ukulele instruction.
Pages 50–51: Twilight casts a
magical glow over Waikīkī,
Diamond Head and Honolulu.

While highly visible, urban Honolulu and Waikīkī are only part of the story of Oʻahu. Though it sometimes would appear that there are more cars than birds here, the island retains an aura that is unique. According to the story that has come down through many centuries, Oʻahu is the result of a tryst between a man and a goddess: Papa the Earth-Mother had only just returned from a visit to Tahiti when she learned that Wākea the Sky-Father had been unfaithful, fathering a series of island-children with the moon goddess Hina. Out of spite, Papa took up with a handsome young lover named Lua. The short (and here somewhat censored) version of this story ends with the birth of the island of Oʻahu.

Though much more mundane, the scientific explanation for Oʻahu's existence is no less fascinating. Like the island of Maui, Oʻahu is the product of volcanic activity by two large shield volcanoes. Estimated to

have first broken the sea's surface several million years ago, lava flowing from both mountains eventually joined to form Oʻahu's large and fertile central plain. Known as the Leilehua Plateau, this large plain is six miles across at its widest point and runs from Waialua on the island's north shore to ʻEwa, the area west of Pearl Harbor on the south shore. Today, due to the forces of erosion working over many eons, the long extinct volcanoes have lost the gradual shield-like shapes for which they are named, and now appear as two separate but roughly parallel mountain ranges, punctuated by numerous peaks, cathedral-shaped valleys and high, jagged pali.

The elder of the two ranges, the Waiʻanae Mountains (part of which—Mount Kaʻala—is the highest point on the island at 4,020 feet), separates the drier west Oʻahu coast from the Leilehua Plateau and the north shore. The younger, lusher Koʻolau range separates the south shore and urban Honolulu from windward Oʻahu—which, like the windward side of all islands, receives the majority of the rain blowing in off the ocean.

Of the main Hawaiian islands, Oʻahu is second only to Kauaʻi in age, and therefore landslides and erosion have played a major part in the shaping of its prominent geographic features. Among the most visibly dramatic of these characteristics is the Nuʻuanu Pali. Stretching for miles and soaring thousands of feet, the Pali, as it is more simply known, serves as a jumping off point between urban Honolulu and the more rural windward side. That is, a jumping off point both figuratively and literally—when Kamehameha landed in Waikīkī in 1795 to challenge the army of chief Kalanikupule, he waged a battle which eventually drove the Oʻahu warriors backwards up to this precipice . . . and over the edge to their deaths.

Above left: *Oʻahu's ʻEwa Plain planted with pineapple.* Opposite: *Two mountain ranges that have evolved from the two shield volcanoes that formed the* island of Oʻahu. Top: *Aerial view, Waiʻanae Mountain range, looking down over leeward Oʻahu.* Bottom: *Dramatic ridges of the Koʻolau Mountains.*

Left: *Aerial view of Diamond Head, Waikīkī and Honolulu.* Above, top: *Koko Head and* *the East Oʻahu coastline.* Bottom: *Punchbowl Crater, National Cemetery of the Pacific.*

Other more recent volcanic activity accounts for some of the most famous sites on Oʻahu. Rising 760 feet and bordering the east end of Waikīkī, Diamond Head was formed approximately 100,000 years ago and is known as a tuff cone—a formation of volcanic ash that has cemented itself together to form solid rock. Likewise, southeast Oʻahu's Koko Head (which houses a unique arboretum) and central Honolulu's Punchbowl (which holds the Punchbowl Memorial of the Pacific) are both relatively young tuff cones.

*Scenes at Hanauma Bay, a
marine life conservation district.*

Another major volcanic feature of Oʻahu is the
famed Hanauma Bay, on the island's southeastern
shore near Koko Head. Once a coastal crater, the ero-
sive force of ocean waves pounding on its southern rim
eventually wore a large section away, creating the
scenic bay that is now a marine sanctuary and prime
snorkeling destination.

Yes, Oʻahu is crowded, but even so, there is a certain
innocence to it all. Most locals simply refer to the
Honolulu area as "Town." And Town is only part of the
story of Oʻahu. "Country" (that is, Oʻahu's famed north
shore) is a Mecca not only for surfers from around the
world seeking what are generally considered to be the

best (and largest) waves on the planet, but also for townies looking to escape the urban landscape for an area closer to the Hawai'i of old.

The island's western shore—which, in another ode to linguistic functionality, is usually just referred to as "West Side"—is home to a large Hawaiian population and a smoother, quieter lifestyle. There's an aura surrounding the Wai'anae coast that no doubt springs in part from its history. It was here that the demigod Maui —always the mix of prankster and benefactor—came to steal fire for humans from a group of crafty mud hens who served as its keeper. And it was here that the conquered O'ahuan's came to live after Kamehameha had vanquished the armies of Kalanikupule. (The leeward coast of all islands being generally arid, Wai'anae was not particularly desirable to the invaders.)

During this period a special school was established by exiled kāhuna (priests) at Pōka'i Bay, located near the center of modern Wai'anae, to preserve the folklore of their O'ahu homeland. Today, Pōka'i is a boat harbor berthing a small fleet of locally-owned fishing boats. (The name Wai'anae, incidentally, points to its heritage as a fishing community: "wai" means water; "anae" is a type of large mullet.)

Left: *Mākua Valley and the Wai'anae Mountains, O'ahu.*

Below: *Surfers and waves, Yokohama Bay, west O'ahu.*

O'ahu's variety. Above: Color-
ful spinnakers, Ala Wai Boat
Harbor. Left: pro surfer Gerry
Lopez, Pipeline Master's Surf
contest, North shore. Below:
Yokohama Bay, Leeward side.
Opposite top: Ko'olau Moun-
tains. Center, left to right:
Hiker on the Maunawili Trail.
Hikers on the Maunawili Trail,
windward side. Couple and rain-
bow on 'Ehukai Beach, North
shore. Bottom: Pu'u O Mahuka
Heiau on O'ahu's North shore.

Above: *Mālaekahana State Park.*
Below: *Waimea Bay.* Opposite
page, top: *Shoreline fishing,*

*Bellows Beach, twin Mokulua
islands in background.* Opposite,
bottom: *Waimānalo Beach.*

Even from the heart of downtown Honolulu, solitude is 10 minutes away in virtually any direction. The hills above town are crisscrossed with a network of picturesque hiking trails, most of which eventually lead more experienced hikers to the cliff's edge of the Ko'olau Mountains and panoramic views of lush windward O'ahu.

And while Honolulu's steel and glass towers blaze in the sun, there are spots throughout the island that point to a very different past. On the north shore, just around the corner from the famed surf break of Waimea Bay and a mile or so up the winding Pūpūkea Road, stand the remains of the ancient Pu'uomahuka heiau. Dedicated to Kū, the god of war, Pu'uomahuka was a *heiau po'okanaka* (a site where human sacrifices were offered to the god). Measuring 575 feet long and 170 feet wide, the heiau has the largest area of any on O'ahu, and legend has it that its dedicatory fires at one time burned hot enough to warm Kaua'i.

Scenes from windward Oʻahu.
Opposite, clockwise from top:
Kaʻaʻawa Beach and Kualoa
Ridge. Horseback riding through
Kaʻaʻawa Valley. Kualoa Ridge
framing Waikāne Valley. Punaluʻu
Art Gallery. Center: Charter
fishing boat, Heʻeia Kea Pier.
This page, clockwise from top:
Volleyball game. Haʻiku Gardens.
Valley of the Temples. Kāneʻohe
Bay in early morning light.

Above, clockwise from top: *Rainbow and palms. The Mission Houses Museum. Bananas and produce, Chinatown. Meat market and shoppers, Chinatown.* Bottom left: *Trolley in Chinatown.* Opposite top: *'Iolani Palace.* Bottom: *Pineapple patterns in Kunia on the 'Ewa Plain.*

Such is the paradox of O'ahu—an island that encompasses everything cosmopolitan and rural. Virtually every day, in the heart of an urban landscape like Honolulu, one sees rainbows arcing over the lush valleys that hem in the downtown area. A walk through the downtown proper yields historic sites that range from the only royal residence in the United States ('Iolani Palace) to the first Congregationalist missionary settlement on O'ahu (the Mission House Museum) to the historic Chinatown district (twice razed by fires near the turn of the 20th century and now a bustling home to markets that sell everything from traditional medicinal

herbs to souvenirs for visitors). A drive from town through the central plains of Oʻahu provides a window into Hawaiʻi's changing economy, where sugar and pineapple once reigned and where other, smaller, agricultural ventures are now being developed to replace the all-but-dead, large-scale plantations.

Standing in the midst of all of this is Oʻahu's incredibly varied population. In the past, some have referred to Hawaiʻi as "The Melting Pot of the Pacific," a designation that is grossly unfair to the many distinct ethnic groups whose cultures are a unique yet integral part of Hawaiʻi's social landscape. At various times through-

Above, left to right: *Aloha Festivities Royal Court. Dancers at Portuguese Fiesta. Bon dance during Obon season.* Right: *Lion dance motions, Chinese New Year's.* Opposite page, clockwise from top left: *Chinese New Year altar and offerings. Japanese bon dance. Lei Day 'ukulele player. Aloha Week Royal Court. Chinese New Year celebration with drums. Lei Day celebrant. Pa'u rider, Kamehameha Day parade.*

out the year, celebrations take place to mark events ranging from Oktoberfest to the anniversary of Filipino independence from Spanish rule. At these times, the children of native Hawaiians, missionaries, sugar laborers (brought in from Japan, China, the Philippines and Portugal in the late 19th and early 20th centuries) and later arrivals all join together to celebrate each other's cultures. When talking about Hawai'i's multi-cultural background, it's far better to point to a rainbow . . . to realize that its beauty comes from its many distinct colors.

Such is O'ahu. An island poised with one foot in the 21st century and the other in a storied past—a past that infuses the lives of everyone . . . from laborers picking pineapples in the red dirt fields of Waialua . . . to musicians performing for visitors in Waikīkī . . . to bankers operating out of ultramodern steel-and-glass high-rises in downtown Honolulu.

DEATH OF A SEAMAN

THE FINAL VOYAGE OF CAPTAIN COOK

KNOWING HOW MUCH EARLY HAWAIIANS revered their gods, it's not at all surprising that they would think that a man who appeared on what to them was a "floating island," arriving during a festival period devoted to a god whose return to earth had long been prophesied, was in fact a god. This, in the end, was to be Captain James Cook's downfall.

By the time he stumbled upon Kaua'i in 1778, the leader of the expedition that would first reveal the existence of the Hawaiian Islands to the western world had already made a name for himself in the annals of navigation. In 1768, Cook had spent six months mapping the coasts of New Zealand and eastern Australia before returning to England via a trip around the world.

On his next voyage, during which he commanded the *Resolution* and *Adventure*, Cook was the first to go south of the Antarctic Circle—in the process documenting the existence of numerous Pacific islands. After sailing a record three years and covering more than 60,000 miles, the *Resolution* returned to England in July, 1775.

Cook's final voyage was only his third, but it completed a decade as the prime *western* explorer of the Pacific. (While Cook's accomplishments were exemplary in European terms, it's important to note that the original residents of the Pacific had already covered most of the same ground hundreds of years earlier, and were far more accomplished seafarers).

For this voyage, Cook commanded the *Resolution*; his consort ship was the *Discovery* under Captain Charles Clerke. After returning briefly to the South Pacific—and noting the existence of Christmas Island—the ships headed northward. On January 18, 1778, the *Resolution* made sight of an island to the northeast, and another to the north. The next day, a third island appeared to the northwest—O'ahu, Kaua'i and Ni'ihau had been "discovered," and Cook christened them the Sandwich Islands after his patron, the Earl of Sandwich.

Captain Cook went ashore for the first time at the village of Waimea, Kaua'i, on January 21, 1778. Here, like everywhere else he would travel in the Hawaiian Islands, he was greeted as if he were one of the highest chiefs. Cook also went ashore a few days later on Ni'ihau.

Trade began with the Hawaiians, aided by the fact that the local language was similar to that spoken by a group of Tahitians who were sailing onboard the *Resolution*. (The similarities in language would later help to confirm the theory that Tahitians were actually the second wave of settlers to arrive in Hawai'i.) The Hawaiians were especially interested in acquiring iron nails, which they fashioned into fishhooks.

Above: *In Kealakekua Bay a kayaker paddles around rocks on his way to the Captain Cook Monument.*
Background: *Low tide exposes lava in the southeast corner of Kealakekua Bay.*

Kids and adults plunge into Alahaka Bay from a lava tube found along the King's Trail in Hōnaunau, Kona Coast of the Big Island. Opposite: A local family enjoys a kayak outing in Honomalino Bay.

Unfortunately, there was other trade. Cook tried in vain to keep the 66 sailors (more than half of the crew of 112) who had measurable cases of venereal disease onboard his ship and away from the native women. But to no avail: when the *Resolution* returned less than a year later, Cook would note that signs of V.D. were already apparent in some Hawaiian faces.

The two ships headed north early in February in search of the mythic Northwest Passage linking the Pacific and Atlantic Oceans through North America. The mariners spent many months exploring the coasts from Oregon on the American side across to Kamchatka on the Asian side, even venturing beyond the Arctic Circle without finding the fabled passage.

Cook decided to sail south to spend the coming winter in the warm and friendly Sandwich Islands.

On November 26, 1778, the ships sighted Maui. Two chiefs who were fighting each other, Kahekili of Maui and Kalaniopu'u of Hawai'i island, visited the ships separately. After eight weeks of searching for a suitable harbor, Cook sailed on to the Big Island. This is where things began to fall apart for him. (An interesting historical aside: While sailing the coast of Maui, one of Cook's lieutenant's made detailed maps. The map maker, William Bligh, would eventually go down in history himself as captain of HMS *Bounty*.)

Cook sailed into Kealakekua Bay, a Big Island port some 20 miles south of modern day Kailua-Kona town, on January 16, 1779, at the height of the makahiki season—a four-month period of sports and religious festivities dedicated to Lono, the fertility god of the earth. It was a long-standing belief that Lono would one day return to the earth and Cook's arrival seemed to fulfill this prophesy. Effigies of Lono normally took the shape of a small wooden figure perched on a tall mast-like crossbeam; long, white sheets of tapa cloth hung down from the crossbeam. In addition, Kealakekua (considered to be Lono's sacred harbor) was the first spot that Cook chose to land, after circling the entire Big Island in search of a harbor. Therefore, he was treated for a time as a god.

After about a month, however, the visitors had begun to wear out their welcome. During this period one of Cook's crew died, proving to the Hawaiians that the visitors were in fact mortal. William Watman's remains were buried at the Hikiau Heiau, which was dedicated to Lono. (Today, a plaque marks the site, just off the Kealakekua Bay parking lot.)

A series of thefts were perpetrated against Cook's vessels, even as members of his crew were unwittingly breaking various *kapu*. Cook finally set sail on February 4, but was forced back into the harbor with a broken mast barely a week later. When a group of Hawaiians stole a small cutter, Cook made what was to be a fatal error in judgment. Going ashore with nine armed men, he tried to convince chief Kalaniopu'u to return to the *Resolution* as ransom for the stolen boat. While Kalaniopu'u debated, another group of sailors fired upon a canoe trying to leave the bay, killing a lower-ranking chief named No'okemai.

At this point, the crowd around Cook had reached several thousand. One brave warrior attacked Cook, striking him with a *pāhoa* (a short dagger). Cook drew a pistol that was lightly loaded and shot back, but the charge bounced harmlessly off the warrior's protective straw-mat armor. The mariners retreated to their landing boat, but Cook could not escape. (The tale goes that Cook died standing in knee-deep water, the legendary navigator who did not know how to swim.)

Eventually a truce was arranged and the ship's mast and parts of Cook's body were returned to the *Resolution*. (As was the custom, other parts had been distributed to various chiefs involved in the fighting.) He was interred in the waters off of Kealakekua Bay.

Today, a 27-foot tall, white marble obelisk stands at the northern end of the bay as a memorial to Captain James Cook—a man who would not only introduce Hawai'i to the outside world, but also forever alter the island nation's history.

THE VALLEY ISLE

GREATER MAUI

THE KUMULIPO sings of the demigod Maui—a half-human trickster whose exploits are known and revered throughout Polynesia. It is said that Maui and his brothers brought the islands of Polynesia into existence by fishing them up from the ocean floor in one heroic tug. Part Prometheus, part Paul Bunyan, it was the prankster Maui who lassoed the sun, forcing it to move more slowly across the sky; Maui who stole fire from a crafty mud hen and gifted it to humankind (nearly setting the world on fire in the process); and Maui who ultimately died at the powerful hands of the goddess Hina.

Fitting then that the only island in Polynesia to bear the name of a god should be the island of Maui—such is its power, beauty and magic. From the lunar desert of east Maui's Haleakalā crater (the largest dormant volcano in the world) to the lush rainforests and bogs of the West Maui Mountains; from the verdant pasture lands of upcountry Maui on Haleakalā's western flank to the sugar white beaches and upscale resorts of Kapalua and Kā'anapali—there are few places in the Pacific that can match Maui's grace and diversity.

Maui is the creation of two separate shield volcanoes—the 10,023-foot tall Haleakalā, which makes up all of east Maui, and the much older West Maui Mountains (the highest point being Pu'u Kukui, at 5,788 feet). The two volcanoes are bridged by an isthmus, created when lava flowing down Haleakalā's eastern flank joined with past eruptions from the West Maui Mountains.

Though Pu'u Kukui (the name translates literally as "candlenut hill") is today dwarfed by the mass of Haleakalā, at one time the shield's crater measured approximately five miles across. Eruptions, collapses and stream erosion have reshaped the entire mountain range, creating a series of spectacular cliffs and canyons that have led Maui to be rightfully nicknamed "The Valley Isle." The famed 'Iao Needle, rising like a finger 2,250 feet above sea level, is actually a remnant of the original Pu'u Kukui caldera, and a product of this natural erosion.

Estimated to be nearly one million years old, Haleakalā is far younger than its West Maui counterpart—which accounts for its much gentler slopes and intact, 7-mile long crater. With a land mass four times that of West Maui, the dormant volcano—which last erupted in the late 1700s—makes up the bulk of the island.

It has been pointed out that, when flying over Maui today, the outline of the island looks much like the torso of a man—or perhaps a demi-god?—gazing down at the island of Kaho'olawe. West Maui in this sense is the island's head, with the fishing village of Kahakuloa at the back of the head, the stretch of beaches between Kapalua and Kā'anapali as the forehead, Olowalu as the nose and Mā'alaea as the base of the chin. The neck—that is, the isthmus—is bounded on the north by Kahului and on the south by Kīhei. The body, with

Above: *Petroglyph at Kukui Point, near Shipwreck Beach, Lāna'i.* Background: *The steep canyon walls of 'Iao Valley.* Opposite top: *Ālau Island as seen from Koki Beach, Hāna.* Opposite bottom: *Scene along busy Front Street in Lahaina at night.* Pages 76–77: *2,250 foot 'Iao Needle, 'Iao Valley State Park.*

Hāna at the easternmost "waist," is made up entirely by the bulk of Haleakalā. For all of Haleakalā's impressive volume and West Maui's craggy valley terrain, at its widest points Maui is a mere 25 miles across from north to south and 40 miles from east to west.

Maui's recent history is as much the stuff of legend as the island's storied namesake was. In 1790, west Maui's Olowalu Beach became the infamous sight of what Hawaiians would come to refer to as "the day of spilled brains," when American sea-captain Simon Metcalfe—enraged over the theft of a small boat and the murder of one of his crew—ordered his men to open fire on a group of islanders whom he had invited out to his vessel. More than 100 people were murdered. Later, in an unrelated incident, Metcalfe managed to insult Kameiamoku, a chief on the island of Hawai'i's Kona coast, who in turn vowed to destroy the next for-eign sailors he saw . . . which turned out to be Metcalfe's son and his five-man crew, sailing the *Fair American* into the same Kona harbor a few days later.

Only the ship's mate, Isaac Davis, was spared as an acknowledgment of his bravery in battle. Later that same year Kamehameha I embarked with Davis aboard the *Fair American* for Hāna, using the east Maui village (and the ship's cannons) as the starting point for a campaign that would eventually unite all of the Hawaiian Islands under one ruler. For a time, west Maui's port of Lahaina would be Kamehameha's royal seat.

By the mid-1800s, Lahaina harbor was the central port of the American whaling fleet; today, it is part of the Humpback Whale National Marine Sanctuary and a prime winter destination for visitors hoping to catch a glimpse of one of these endangered giants.

Things change and things remain the same. Like all

Opposite: *Cinder cone in Haleakalā Crater, Maui.*

Above: *West Maui Mountains and ʻĪao Valley from Spreckelsville.*

of Hawaiʻi, the Aloha spirit is alive in Maui's residents, linking the upcountry farmer in Kula growing onions that are renowned as the sweetest in the world, to the artist hawking his wares on a Saturday afternoon in Lahaina, shaded by one of the world's largest banyan trees. This is the true source of Maui's magic.

Today, visitors to the island can choose between stays in five-star west Maui resorts or visits to east Maui's Hāna (often called "the most Hawaiian spot" in the island chain) or even to Kahakuloa—the nearly inaccessible north Maui fishing village said to be a favorite destination of the demigod himself. The island's nearshore waters are home to some of the best surfing and windsurfing in the world. The tiny, crescent-shaped Molokini island, a three-mile boat ride from Maui's southwest shore, is a popular day-sailing desti-

nation and both Molokaʻi and Lānaʻi are short plane hops away. Adventurous hikers can spend the night in one of three cabins in the Haleakalā National Park. The less adventurous can spend an evening taking in the night life sights of Lahaina. Truly, Maui is a land of many faces.

Technically speaking, Maui is also somewhat larger than it would first appear. While the land bridges linking Maui, Molokaʻi, Lānaʻi and Kahoʻolawe were submerged by rising sea levels millennia ago, the islands continue to be linked in a much more mundane fashion. What was once known as Maui Nui is now Maui County. Of Maui's three neighbors, only two—Molokai and Lānaʻi—are populated. The third, Kahoʻolawe, is presently uninhabitable. Though each island is a short hop from Maui, each has a distinct geography and history that belies any common past.

An admission—to say that Maui is the only island in Polynesia named after a god is a misstatement.

Above: *The Visitors Center overlooks Haleakalā crater.*
Left: *Hikers arriving at Palikū cabin in the crater.*
Below: *Nēnē geese (Hawai'i's state bird) inside the crater.*
Opposite: *Packing in supplies on the Halemau'u trail, Haleakalā.*
Pages 84–85: *Lahaina Harbor.*

Better to say that it is the only island *currently* named after a god. Kahoʻolawe was originally known as Kanaloa, in honor of one of the four major Hawaiian deities and a divinity much revered by kāhuna ʻanāʻanā (priests who practiced black magic). Created, according to Hawaiian cosmology, by the union of Wākea and Papa, Kahoʻolawe became the center of a disagreement between two goddesses, and is said to have been cursed into desolation . . . a curse that has been borne out time and again over the centuries.

In the early 1800s, Queen Kaahumanu banished criminals to the island; by the 1860s, goats and sheep were running slipshod over the native vegetation. In 1910, the Territory of Hawaiʻi named the entire island a forest reserve, but little was done to protect it—with one exception. In 1917, rancher Angus McPhee attempted to initiate a reforestation effort, planting thousands of native trees and eucalyptus windbreaks and—in one year—removing and selling some 13,000 goats.

A good start, but a failed effort ultimately. At the advent of World War II, the U.S. Navy took possession of Kahoʻolawe, and through 1990 used the island as a bombing target, severely altering the landscape and leaving a legacy that will be years in the undoing.

The island of Molokaʻi stands in grand contrast to Kahoʻolawe's fate. With the exception of Niʻihau (a privately-owned island where traditional Hawaiian ways are still adhered to and access by outsiders is strictly limited), Molokaʻi is literally the most Hawaiian of all the islands. It is the only other island in the Hawaiian chain where people of Hawaiian ancestry make up the majority of the population.

Once an island of refuge for defeated warriors and those who had broken the laws of the kapu system, like all Polynesian places of refuge Molokaʻi was protected

not by brute strength but by the chants of kāhuna and by the land's own mana — that is, its life force. Today, that power is manifested not only in an island that has managed to remain relatively rural, but in a people who are fiercely committed to preserving a vanishing way of life. Though the lights of Oʻahu are brightly visible from the western shores of the island and there is much pressure from developers hoping to heighten Molokaʻi's

appeal to visitors, there are currently no traffic lights, no fast food restaurants and no movie theaters. One has to wonder what could be more appealing.

What Molokaʻi *does* have is a storied past and an unparalleled natural beauty. North Molokaʻi's Kalaupapa, a peninsula bounded on one side by the ocean and on the other by a 1,500-foot pali, was the site of a leper colony where those suffering from the disease were exiled to die. This was where Joseph De Veuster, otherwise known as Father Damien, landed in 1873 on his selfless mission to bring hope to the colony. Today, Kalaupapa's residents—all former patients—live on the peninsula of their own free will, leading an occasional tour for visitors willing to brave the walk or donkey ride from above.

To the east of Kalaupapa the pali rises even higher,

Opposite page, top: *Kahoʻolawe.*
Bottom: *The Garden of the Gods,*
Lānaʻi, Molokaʻi in the distance.

Above: *An upcountry Maui*
view of late afternoon sun setting
over Kahoʻolawe and Molokini.

Pages 86–87: *The cliffs along*
the northern coast of Molokaʻi
are among the world's highest.

topping 1,750 feet at Kahiwa Falls—the spot that marks the world's tallest sea cliff. Directly south, on the other side of the island, lies Kaunakakai—at three blocks long, the island's main town. Driving highway 450 east from Kaunakakai gives a magnificent tour back into old Hawai'i, as ancient fishponds, heiau (temples) and more recent churches drift slowly past. The road eventually leads to Hālawa Valley, once the site of a small but thriving community that moved on after a 1946 tsunami destroyed most of the area's homes and taro fields. Today, Hālawa is for the most part uninhabited, and features easy hikes to waterfalls, ponds and a beach where the valley opens up to the ocean.

Lāna'i too is an island of many stories. Once a for-saken land believed to be inhabited by flesh-eating spirits, the 140 square-mile island is said to have been cleared of the evil beings by Prince Kaululaau, who tricked the ghouls into leaving after he was exiled to the island. Today Lāna'i is best known as the "Pineapple Island"—an apt name considering the island was once home to the largest pineapple plantation in the world.

Maui Nui, the name assigned to the original island of Maui, can be translated as "Great Maui"—a phrase that holds true for each of the islands that once made up this large landmass. Each is now separated by both ocean and history, and yet all are linked by a certain subtle heritage: all are members of a long-standing, close knit family. Such is Maui.

Opposite left: *The cemetery at St. Philomena, Father Damien's church, at Kalawao, Moloka'i.*
Opposite right: *Waterfalls abound along the precipitous northern coast of Moloka'i.*
Right: *Beginning snorkelers enjoy the calm waters in this tide pool at Mānele Bay, Lāna'i.*

THE 50TH STATE?
FROM KINGDOM TO STATEHOOD

THOUGH CAPTAIN COOK'S ARRIVAL signaled the beginning of a new and challenging era for Hawai'i, the real significance of his chancing upon the islands would only begin to show with another set of arrivals some 40 years later. In 1819, American ships caught a whale off the coast of the island of Hawai'i—the first to be caught in the islands; in 1820, the first of the American Protestant missionaries arrived in the Kingdom.

Significantly, Kamehameha I, the warrior-chief who had unified all of the islands under his rule and had staunchly resisted any outside attempts to supplant traditional Hawaiian religious practices, died on May 8, 1819. The death of Hawai'i's first king came at a time when the old religion was no longer secure, particularly the kapu system. This was a complex system of taboos governing many aspects of Hawaiian life and regulating everything from the foods that could be eaten to the ways in which different members of the community could interact with each other.

The penalty for breaking the kapu was often death, which was accepted as a punishment meted out by the gods. However, increased contact with Europeans had

thrown the kapu system into doubt. It had become quickly obvious that the Europeans could break the kapu at will, without fear of punishment by the gods. Eventually, Kamehameha's son Liholiho, reigning as Kamehameha II, would yield to pressure exerted upon him by two of Kamehameha's wives—Kaahumanu and Liholiho's mother Keopuolani—to break the kapu through a public feast, in which men ate with women and foods that were traditionally forbidden women were served.

The breakdown of the kapu system, coinciding with the arrival of missionaries and the increased Western presence due to the whaling industry, led to large-scale changes in Hawaiian society. Approximately 30 percent of the population of Hawai'i would be claimed as members of the church by 1853. During this same period, the missionaries were gaining ever increasing influence in government—an influence which they seemed to believe was best exerted by trying to make as many of the Kingdom's institutions as American as possible.

This led to changes which many Hawaiians were not culturally equipped to understand. Beginning in

Above: *Hawaiian ki'i akua (deity images) surround Hale o Keawe Heiau, at Pu'uhonua o Hōnaunau National Historic Park on the island of Hawai'i.*
Background: *A winter sunset silhouettes the ki'i at the Place of Refuge.*

the mid-1840s, private land ownership was instituted for the first time in Hawai'i, as the kingdom abandoned the traditional ahupua'a system—a system in which land was divided into large pieces that ran from the mountain to the sea, providing all of the resources necessary for a community's survival. In place of the ahupua'a came the "Great Mahele" (the "Great Division"), in which lands were reapportioned between the crown, government, chiefs and commoners.

Contact with Westerners had brought with it a number of diseases that had drastically affected the Hawaiian population. One century after Cook's arrival in Hawai'i, the native Hawaiian population had shrunk from an estimated 300,000 to 45,000, due mainly to the effects of cholera, venereal diseases, smallpox and leprosy.

Sugar cane fields viewed through wild bougainvillea in Spreckelsville on Maui.

Unfortunately, what was originally believed by the Hawaiian monarchy to be a benefit for commoners turned out to be a disaster. By 1850, it was possible for foreigners to buy land in fee simple. This, combined with the fact that most Hawaiians had only the vaguest understanding of the concept of personal land ownership, led to a virtual eviction of the majority of native Hawaiians from their own land.

By the late 1840s the sugar industry was also beginning to play a major part in the shaping of Hawai'i.

A side effect of this loss was the need to import outside laborers to work the cane fields—a process that began in 1852 with the first boatload of Chinese laborers and would in time include workers from Japan, Portugal, the Philippines and Europe.

Eventually, sugar interests would also lead to the forcible overthrow of the Hawaiian Monarchy. Though for a time Hawai'i enjoyed a reciprocity treaty with the United States that allowed sugar to be exported to America without tariff, in 1890 the United States replaced its sugar tariff policy with a bounty that was paid for sugar grown in the United States. Hawaiian sugar had thus lost its advantage, and the

was meant to determine the will of the native people, voters were given the choice of remaining annexed to the United States or becoming the newest state in the union. The end result of this vote was that Hawaiʻi became the 50th state and, as a member of the United States, was removed from the United Nations list of "non self-governing nations"—that is, nations that were scheduled to be decolonized and returned to self-rule under the UN charter.

The vote was for statehood. However, because U.S. military personnel residing on bases in Hawaiʻi were allowed to vote and the only options given were choices among two types of U.S.-governance (the UN charter states that a true plebiscite must allow for all options, including self-governance), many Hawaiian sovereignty activists today claim that this process was at the very least flawed . . . and quite possibly illegal.

Left: *Plaque in front of Washington Place, the Governor's mansion, commemorating Liliʻuokalani and "Aloha ʻOe," the song she wrote.*

Below: *Statue of Queen Liliʻuokalani, which stands between the former royal palace and the new State Capitol.*

industry was plunged into a depression that fueled a growing annexationist movement among the sugar growers and other non-Hawaiians who were frustrated with a lack of voice in the Hawaiian government.

This movement would eventually lead to a U.S.-backed revolt and overthrow of the reigning monarch, Liliʻuokalani, on January 17, 1893. In July of 1898, in part due to the increasing presence of the United States in the Pacific via the Spanish-American war, Hawaiʻi was annexed. On August 12 of that year, amid cheers from the annexationists and tears of many native Hawaiians, the flag of Hawaiʻi was brought down from its position over ʻIolani Palace, cut into small strips and distributed throughout the gathered crowd as a memento of the day.

A little more than 60 years later, on August 21, 1959, Hawaiʻi would become a member of the United States. In a vote mandated by the United Nations that

THE BIG ISLAND
THE ISLAND OF HAWAI'I

Lt's said that the reason half of the island of Hawai'i is lush while the other half is arid is because of an encounter between the volcano goddess Pele and Kamapua'a—a shape-shifting demigod who most often manifests himself as a boar (that is, a *pua'a*).

According to the story, Kamapua'a one day came to the edge of Halema'uma'u, the giant crater on the slopes of Kīlauea volcano where Pele and her sisters to this day reside. As Kamapua'a stood on the rim of the crater, Pele's sisters looked up and exclaimed:

"Pele, there is a handsome warrior standing up there on the edge of the pali!"

But when Pele—who most often takes the shape either of a beautiful young woman or a wizened grandmother—looked up, that's not what she saw.

"Warrior!" She laughed. "All I see is a smelly pig!"

Hearing this, Kamapua'a looked down and said, "Well, all I see is a shriveled old hag!"

And so began a battle. Pele hurling molten lava into the skies and Kamapua'a, who had powers over the weather, summoning the rains in an attempt to drown Pele's fires. In the end, the two fought to a standoff . . . and came to an agreement. Pele would take one half of the island, and Kamapua'a the other. Eventually, the two would also take each other as lovers.

So it is that the leeward side of Hawai'i—in general, the area to the west of Mauna Loa and Mauna Kea vol-canoes—is for the most part dry, while the windward, eastern side of the island is much wetter. (Hilo, the capital city of the island and the second most populous area in the Hawaiian chain, receives an average of 150 inches of rain per year.)

But nothing about the Big Island, as the largest and youngest of the major Hawaiian islands is known, is so cut and dried. Virtually every type of geographic formation, terrain and climate to be found on earth can be found on this one island. There are rain forests and deserts here, snow-white beaches and snow-capped mountains. In a day, one can travel from sea level to above the cloud level, at the summit of Mauna Kea.

At 4,038 square miles, the island of Hawai'i is large enough to house all of the other major Hawaiian islands combined. The island is made up of five large shield volcanoes. The tallest, Mauna Kea ("snow mountain"), rises 13,796 feet above the sea. The others are Mauna Loa ("long mountain"—13,677 feet), Hualālai (8,271 feet), Kohala (5,480 feet) and Kīlauea (4,093 feet). Kīlauea, which has been erupting almost continuously since 1983, and Mauna Loa (which last erupted for 22 days in March of 1984 and sent lava flowing to within four miles of the outskirts of Hilo) are active volcanoes. Mauna Kea and Kohala are considered to be extinct, having last erupted many hundreds of years ago. Hualālai falls between these two categories. Since it last

Above: The summit of Mauna Kea rises 13,796 feet above downtown Hilo. *Background:* Palms of Mauna Kea Beach Hotel's golf course entrance frame Mauna Kea. *Opposite top:* Ice covered snow depth-gauge is a reminder that the weather can be fierce atop Mauna Kea. *Opposite bottom:* Sunbather relaxes at Hāpuna Beach Park.

A hiker views the huge steam cloud created by the lava flow to the Pacific. Opposite, clockwise from top left: Hot pāhoehoe lava forms unusual patterns on a cliff above the ocean. Older flows dot the prehistoric landscape near Halemaʻumaʻu Crater. Lava closeup shows the unusual color found on this "tree mold." Another tree mold illustrates how fragile and glasslike lava can be.

erupted somewhere around the year 1800, it still must be considered to be dormant—that is, sleeping.

The size of the island and wide range in elevations make for an incredibly diverse climate. Certain areas on the windward (eastern) slopes of Mauna Loa have rainfall that tops 300 inches annually. Meanwhile the leeward coast is shielded by the mountains from the rain clouds that are blown in off the ocean by the prevailing northeasterly tradewinds. Some areas of this region are so dry that they are classified as true desert. At the summits of both Mauna Kea and Mauna Loa, snow often falls during the winter months.

Like the youth that it is, the island is still incredibly active. The erupting volcanoes occasionally trigger earthquakes. Most are minor, but not always. On

November 29, 1975, much of the island's Puna coast subsided (literally dropping several feet in an instant), triggering an earthquake that topped 7 on the Richter scale.

In the area of the oldest flows, the Kohala Mountains, the lava has long broken down into extremely fertile soil, with the upper reaches of the mountains blanketed in lush rain forest. However, where fresher flows have occurred, geologists and volcanists have a unique opportunity to literally reenact the creation of the earth. Lava in Hawaiʻi takes on two unique forms, rough and jagged clinker lava (ʻaʻā) and smooth, ropy and wrinkled lava (pāhoehoe). (An interesting note: Because Hawaiʻi has been so prominent in the advance of volcanology, these two terms have become the universal descriptions worldwide for these types of lava flows).

Above left: *Hikers stroll across
the floor of Kīlauea Iki Crater.*
Right: *Steaming Bluffs is active
when surface water hits hot
rocks just below ground level.*
Opposite: *At sunset spectators
watch lava explode when it
empties into the Pacific Ocean.*

Scenes from Hilo, the Big Island.
Clockwise from top left:
*King Kalākaua bronze statue.
Hulihuli chicken barbecue.
Tsunami (May 1960) memorial
clock. Wailuku River bridge fisherman. Flower leis for sale at the
Hilo farmers' market. Chinese
vegetable stand. A fish merchant
sells his catch. Fishing boats are
moored in the Wailoa River next
to Suisan Market. A vendor dis-
plays locally grown fresh flowers.*

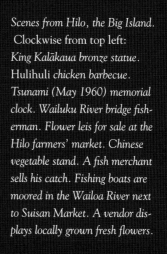

Clockwise from top left: Anthuriums at the farmers' market. King Kamehameha statue with leis. Kīlauea Preserve Center and shop owner. Haili Church (1859) exterior and interior views. Kamehameha Avenue and the Koehnen Building. Suisan fish auction, held every morning except Sundays at 7:30 a.m. Suisan Market dock. Fishermen at the teahouse, Lili'uokalani Gardens.

Each of the island's nine districts has a flavor of its own. South Hilo, on the eastern slopes of Mauna Loa and Mauna Kea, houses the town of Hilo proper, with its low, false-front buildings straight out of a Hollywood Western (much of the downtown area has a two-story height restriction). North Hilo encompasses the southern Hāmākua Coast—a largely agri-

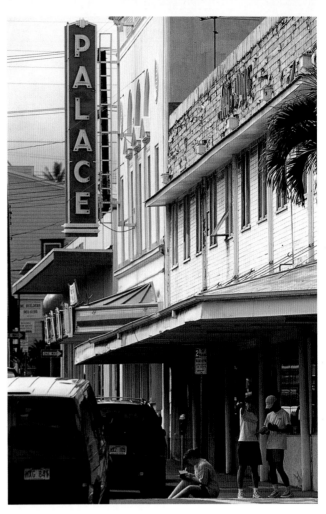

Above left: *The refurbished 1912 Hata Building, downtown Hilo.* Above: *The old Palace Theater, on Haili Street, Hilo.* Left: *In a very calm sea, a lone kayaker paddles by Waimanu Valley on the Hāmākua Coast.* Opposite top: *Pololū Valley and the northeast Kohala Coast.* Opposite, bottom left: *Kamaʻoa Beach from Mauna Kea Beach Hotel on Kohala's "Gold Coast."* Opposite, bottom right: *The Kona Inn Restaurant, downtown Kailua-Kona, on a windy day.*

cultural area once dominated by hundreds of acres of sugar cane fields, though now increasingly home to smaller farming ventures. The district of Hāmākua stretches inland from the northern section of the Hāmākua coast up to the summit of Mauna Kea and north along the coast, enclosing most of the string of seven majestic valleys that begins with Waipiʻo in the south and ends with Pololū in the north. North Kohala, the landmass created by the Kohala volcano (the island's oldest) boasts the tiny rural town of Hāwī (pop.

924), and cool and wet agricultural lands. South Kohala contains the town of Waimea (at one time home to the world's largest privately owned cattle ranch); the seaport of Kawaihae; the famed resorts and pristine beaches of the island's "Gold Coast" and the long expanses of barren lava fields that stretch to the northern portion of Kona town. North Kona is home to Kailua-Kona, another popular tourist destination. Puʻuhonua ʻo Hōnaunau National Park (sometimes referred to as the City of Refuge) and Kealakekua Bay, the site of Captain James Cook's death, are found in South Kona. The district of Kaʻū is best known for Ka Lae (South Point), the southernmost tip of the United States and an area that is home to the lesser known natural wonder of Green Sands Beach. The tiny, former plantation towns of Nāʻālehu and Pāhala are also found here, as is the Kaʻū Desert. The Puna District shares Volcanoes National Park with Kaʻū, as well as encasing the Puna coastline, which was home to a number of small settlements known collectively as

back doors unlocked. Their homes have been built on paths used by the Night Marchers, legendary spirits who walk the same path over and over, and whose look can kill . . . and who will bang incessantly on doors that bar their way.

Tales abound of the mischievous works of spirits on the Saddle Road, which connects Hilo to Waimea and the Kona coast by cutting between Mauna Loa and Mauna Kea. Hunters know that carrying pork on this road without leaving a proper offering is an invitation for trouble.

Kalapana before most of the area was inundated by Pele's lava in the 1980s.

More than any other island, Hawai'i retains much of the island chain's mythic past. Ancient heiau (temples) can still be found at numerous sites throughout the island, as can petroglyphs—rock carvings that tell the story of Hawai'i's first inhabitants. Ancient rock walls, pieced together by hand without any mortar, can still be seen throughout South Kohala, many to this day being used as property markers for the area's modern settlers.

And there is also a more palpable presence here. In the Keaukaha area, just outside of Hilo town, certain homeowners have learned to leave their front and

Opposite top: Pu'ukoholā Heiau National Historic Site is dwarfed by snow-capped Mauna Kea. Opposite bottom: Lapakahi State Historic Site recreates a fishing village of about 1300 A.D. Above: Puakō petroglyph site, one of the state's largest, on the Big Island's Kohala Coast. Right: 'Anaeho'omalu petroglyph field.

Opposite: Waterfall
on the Big Island's
Hāmākua Coast.
Above left: *Hiʻilawe
Falls, Waipiʻo Valley.*
Right: *Wailoa Stream
in Waipiʻo Valley.*

And of course there is Pele, one of the first to arrive in the Hawaiian Islands and one of the longest enduring of the chain's otherworldly inhabitants. It is not enough to say that people believe in the legend of Pele. She is here simultaneously as creator—adding many new acres of land to the island—and destroyer, burying numerous homes and countless ancient archeological sites in the Puna district since 1983.

The tale of Pele is one of the most enduring in the Hawaiian islands, having survived even when virtually every other deity was cast out with the kapu system in 1819. Obviously, this is because her presence is still visible to this day. After an especially large eruptive phase, thin, gray-white strands of volcanic glass are

occasionally blown into the sky, often settling many miles from the eruption site—this is known as Pele's hair. In areas closer to the actual lava flow, small, highly-polished droplets of lava sometimes harden separately from the regular flow—these are Pele's tears.

The story begins with Pele's migration from the land of Polapola (aka Bora Bora), through the northwest Hawaiian islands and on down the chain. Moving from island to island, Pele would dig with her magical ʻōʻō stick (a spear-like digging implement), trying to create a suitable home for herself and her sisters and brothers. In the end, it was only at Halemaʻumaʻu, on the slopes of Kīlauea volcano, that Pele was able to dig a hole deep enough to house her fires—a pit over 1,300 feet deep. It was here that Pele established her permanent home, in one of the world's most active volcanoes, situated within the boundaries of what is today known as the Hawai'i Volcanoes National Park.

Here she remains, one of the most powerful figures in natural history and world mythology—and one of the most paradoxical. On the one hand, Pele is recognized as a wrathful goddess; one who is quick to anger and send her destructive lava flowing. On the other hand, it is Pele who protects those who respect her domain . . . and who continues to give birth to new lands.

This is also the paradox and the beauty of the Big Island—a land that has existed for millennia, and yet is still suffering through the process of being born. It is a land that is very much alive.

Opposite: Molten lava from Pu'u 'Ō'ō vent drops into the Pacific. Below: Fiery red and orange lava explodes along the sea cliffs. Right: Devastation Trail, Volcanoes National Park.

THE ALOHA STATE

HAWAI'I IS MANY THINGS to many people. To the banker, it is an urban landscape dominated by the metropolis of Honolulu; to the farmer it might be the upcountry slopes of Kula, Maui or the red dirt fields of Waialua on O'ahu. For visitors it could be the bustle of Waikīkī or the remoteness of Kaua'i's Nā Pali coast or even the desolate lava fields that make up the Ka'ū desert on the Big Island. For Hawai'i residents, it is all of these things.

It is a land of paradoxes, where modern high-rises share the soil with ancient heiau; a haunting place where a volcano goddess still walks the land. It is a world unto itself where, isolated by thousands of miles of ocean, people of virtually every ethnicity, economic standing and religious background have found a way to coexist.

In the simplest of terms, Hawai'i is the 50th state, but there is nothing simple about this statement. Hawai'i is like no other part of the United States, and many today would argue that Hawai'i shouldn't be a part of the United States. Perhaps the simplest and easiest way to circumvent this whole question is to say that Hawai'i exists as its own special state—or rather, in its own special state…a state of Aloha.

Clockwise from left: Canoe paddlers with Diamond Head in the background, O'ahu.
Sunset over Kalalau Valley, Kaua'i. Precipice overlooking Haleakalā crater, Maui.
Jacob and Angel Mau, father and daughter from the island of Maui.
Background: Kahiko hula dancer silhouetted against a sunset sky.
Page 112: Young dancers celebrate Lei Day (top).
Smiling hula dancer from O'ahu (bottom).